Blue Banner Biography

Cole Hamels

Claire O'Neal

Mitchell Lane

PUBLISHERS

P.O. Box 196
Hockessin, Delaware 19707
Visit us on the web: www.mitchelllane.com
Comments? email us: mitchelllane@mitchelllane.com

Mitchell Lane
PUBLISHERS

Printing   1   2   3   4   5   6   7   8   9

Blue Banner Biographies

Akon	Alan Jackson	Alicia Keys
Allen Iverson	Ashanti	Ashlee Simpson
Ashton Kutcher	Avril Lavigne	Bernie Mac
Beyoncé	Bow Wow	Brett Favre
Britney Spears	Carrie Underwood	Chris Brown
Chris Daughtry	Christina Aguilera	Christopher Paul Curtis
Ciara	Clay Aiken	**Cole Hamels**
Condoleezza Rice	Corbin Bleu	Daniel Radcliffe
David Ortiz	Derek Jeter	Eminem
Eve	Fergie (Stacy Ferguson)	50 Cent
Gwen Stefani	Ice Cube	Jamie Foxx
Joe Flacco	John Legend	Ja Rule
Jay-Z	Jennifer Lopez	Jessica Simpson
J. K. Rowling	Johnny Depp	JoJo
Justin Berfield	Justin Timberlake	Kanye West
Kate Hudson	Keith Urban	Kelly Clarkson
Kenny Chesney	Kristen Stewart	Lance Armstrong
Leona Lewis	Lil Wayne	Lindsay Lohan
Mariah Carey	Mario	Mary J. Blige
Mary-Kate and Ashley Olsen	Miguel Tejada	Missy Elliott
Nancy Pelosi	Natasha Bedingfield	Nelly
Orlando Bloom	P. Diddy	Paris Hilton
Peyton Manning	Pink	Queen Latifah
Rihanna	Ron Howard	Rudy Giuliani
Sally Field	Sean Kingston	Selena
Shakira	Shontelle Layne	Soulja Boy Tell 'Em
Taylor Swift	T.I.	Timbaland
Tim McGraw	Toby Keith	Usher
Vanessa Anne Hudgens	Zac Efron	

Library of Congress Cataloging-in-Publication Data
O'Neal, Claire.
   Cole Hamels / by Claire O'Neal.
      p. cm. — (Blue banner biographies)
   Includes bibliographical references and index.
   ISBN 978-1-58415-776-2 (library bound)
   1. Hamels, Cole, 1983–Juvenile literature. 2. Baseball players—United States—Biography—Juvenile literature. 3. Pitchers (Baseball)—United States—Biography—Juvenile literature. I. Title.
   GV865.H235O54 2009
   796.357092--dc22
   [B]
                                                                                              2009004521

ABOUT THE AUTHOR: A versatile author, Claire O'Neal has published several books with Mitchell Lane, including *Extreme Snowboarding with Lindsey Jacobellis*. Claire grew up in the Midwest rooting for the St. Louis Cardinals. She now lives in Delaware, close enough to hear those rowdy Phillies fans cheering for Cole Hamels. Claire enjoys watching sports, especially football, with her husband and two young sons.

PLB

Blue Banner Biography

Chapter 1
The Making of a Changeup Master 5

Chapter 2
Something to Prove 10

Chapter 3
All Eyes on Hollywood 15

Chapter 4
Every Little Leaguer's Dream 20

Chapter 5
What's Next for Cole Hamels? 24

Chronology 29

Further Reading 30

Works Consulted 30

On the Internet 31

Index 32

*Cole Hamels pitches against the Tampa Bay Devil
Rays in Game 1 of the 2008 World Series on October
22. Cole earned a win as the Phillies outscored the
Rays 3-2.*

The Making of a Changeup Master

On June 4, 2002, the Philadelphia Phillies selected their first-round draft pick—a lanky, left-handed high school kid from California. The Phillies knew that Cole Hamels was a bit of a gamble. He pitched for the nation's best high school team, but his own career was marred by a major injury. And Cole wasn't like most of the big-league, beefy lefties winning games with overpowering fastballs. Instead, Cole's specialty was a slow, "old-school" pitch called a changeup. But Phillies scouts were confident in their choice. At eighteen years old, Cole was already an expert in outthinking his batters.

Colbert Michael Hamels was born on December 27, 1983, in San Diego, California, the first of three children born to Amanda and Gary Hamels. Cole, his sister, Jillian, and his brother, Mitchell, grew up in a nice neighborhood in the San Diego suburbs. Good values were important to their parents, who were both educators. They wanted their kids to be honest and decent people, to work hard and treat others with respect. Their respect was important to Cole, too. Even today, Cole says, "My dad still threatens to ground me."

Gary Hamels introduced Cole to sports at an early age. An athletic kid, Cole was a natural at soccer and baseball. He excelled in competitive youth leagues that traveled all over Southern California. When he practiced at home, the neighbors would occasionally complain to Amanda Hamels that Cole had hit their house, car, or even child with a ball. Cole's protests of "I didn't mean to hit him" didn't fly with his mother. Amanda knew that her son already had a powerful, accurate arm.

When he wasn't playing or doing homework, Cole loved watching sports on TV. His sports hero was San Diego Padres pitcher Trevor Hoffman. Hoffman was considered a master of the changeup, which is a pitch designed to fake out the batter. To throw a changeup, the pitcher pretends to throw a regular fastball, but places his fingers differently on the baseball as it leaves his hand. The changeup slows down or changes direction as it nears the plate. If a batter expects a fastball, he will swing too early. Cole would watch in awe as Hoffman pretended to throw fastballs that, like magic, would slow down just in time to make a batter whiff. In an interview on the Major League Baseball web site, Cole said, "I learned early on that deception is a pitcher's best weapon." Hoffman inspired Cole to focus on   baseball, especially pitching.

After Meadowbrook Middle School, Cole attended Rancho Bernardo High School

Cole with his parents, Amanda and Gary Hamels, at Citizens Bank Park

Cole's Little League team in 1996 was also called the Phillies.

in San Diego. The baseball program at Rancho Bernardo is famously called "The Factory." Many skilled, professional-quality athletes have come out of Rancho Bernardo. One famous graduate is Hank Blalock, third baseman for the Texas Rangers and a former All-Star. Blalock's uncle Sam is Rancho Bernardo's baseball coach.

In the spring of 1999, Cole pitched for the Rancho Bernardo freshman baseball team. He was just one of many good pitchers — good, not great. Cole kept company with an elite group. Major League scouts showed up with radar guns even for team practices, clocking fastballs from Cole's young superstar teammates to see who could throw the fastest.

Cole could throw a fastball, but so could everybody else on the team. He told his pitching coach, Mark Furtak, that he wanted to learn a new skill, something that would make him stand out. Furtak taught him how to throw a changeup, just like Trevor Hoffman. As Cole worked hard to learn the new pitch, he came to understand the changeup in a way few pitchers ever do. Many professional pitchers can throw changeups, but when they do, they usually make some involuntary body movement that gives the trick away. Cole is a changeup master because he pitches it from the exact same arm position and uses the same arm speed as his fastball. Hitters, coaches, and even professional baseball analysts can't tell the difference, even on video.

As Cole worked hard to learn the new pitch, he came to understand the changeup in a way few pitchers ever do.

With his new pitch, Cole started striking out hitters in droves. By the spring of 2000, Cole became the number-two starter for the varsity team. He won 11 games and lost only 1, striking out 59 batters over 57 innings pitched. Scouts from the San Diego Padres came calling, impressed with Cole's perfection of not one but two pitches — the tricky changeup and a 94-mph fastball. Thanks in part to Cole's amazing arm, the Rancho Bernardo team won the national high school championship that year. Cole's

When Cole throws his famous circle changeup, he makes a circle with his thumb and index finger to grip the ball. The other three fingers sit behind the ball and power the pitch.

coach told interviewer Mark Tennis, "I've seen a lot of pitchers in San Diego . . . but no one has been better than Cole."

All that changed a few months later. During a game of summer league baseball, Cole threw a fastball that finished high above the batter's head. Hearing a snap like a breaking twig, everyone gasped and looked at Cole's weirdly dangling pitching arm.

Cole had broken his left humerus, or upper arm bone, in two places. It was an unusual injury for a pitcher. Only three Major League pitchers had sustained the same injury, and none of them had ever pitched professionally again.

Something to Prove

Cole and his family consulted the San Diego Padres' team doctor, Dr. Jan Fronek, for treatment. Dr. Fronek recommended major surgery. He placed two metal rods the size of coat hangers in Cole's bone to hold it straight while it healed. He then told Cole to start playing another position, or even to look for another sport. "I took that information as motivation," Cole said in the Major League Baseball web site interview. "It gave me something to prove." Or, as Gary Hamels said, Cole was "just stubborn."

Cole worked hard with pitching coach Tom House to exercise and develop his arm during his slow and painful recovery. He did play baseball his junior year, batting and playing outfield to stay fresh. MLB pitcher Tony Saunders, who had broken his pitching arm twice and was still playing, called Cole personally to encourage him. Luckily, Cole's young age gave him a better chance at recovery, because his arm bones were growing while they were healing. But many MLB scouts begin serious negotiations during a recruit's junior year, and Cole was missing out.

Cole was ready to pitch again almost exactly a year after breaking his arm. Ten to fifteen curious Major League scouts turned up to watch his first game back. Those who had given up on him were in for a surprise: Cole struck out ten batters over five innings. He hurled 92-mph fastballs and tricked batters with his signature changeup. Cole Hamels was back, and better than ever.

Cole's senior season proved to be his best yet, with 10 wins, no losses, and a mind-blowing 0.39 ERA (earned-run average). He also struck out 130 batters in 71 innings. Cole entered the 2002 Major League draft and was picked up in the first round by the Philadelphia Phillies. He graduated from Rancho Bernardo on June 13, 2002, with a contract to begin his career with the Phillies' minor league teams.

Eighteen-year-old Cole dons a Phillies cap at a news conference on August 28, 2002. After two months of negotiations with the team, Cole signed his MLB contract on August 23.

To stay healthy, Cole runs, stretches, does sit-ups, and practices yoga. He credits deep-tissue massage with keeping him limber and injury-free. He prefers vitamins over the medications usually given to pitchers, and drinks water or green tea instead of soda and sports drinks.

In 2003, Cole started with the BlueClaws, the Phillies' single-A team in Lakewood, New Jersey. He impressed the organization right away with 115 strikeouts and another unbelievable ERA of 0.84, and was promoted to the advanced-A Threshers in Clearwater, Florida, later in the season. At the end of the season, Hamels dominated Minor League batters, racking up 147 strikeouts in 101 innings with a 1.34 ERA.

Just when Cole seemed destined for a promotion to the majors, injury struck again. This time, a nagging elbow injury caused him to miss most of the 2004 season. He was ready to play for the 2005 season, but just before it began, Cole broke his pitching hand in a fight at a Florida bar. His hand healed, but he pitched only three games before badly hurting his back. He spent the rest of the season in pain and on the bench. At only 21 years old, constantly fighting injury, he wondered if he might be at the end of his career.

Frustrated with the same old treatment of pills and physical therapy from team doctors, Cole tried something different. He started seeing Dr. Christopher Dugaf, a chiropractor. When Cole first met Dugaf, he hadn't been able to run for three years. Dr. Dugaf recalled to reporter Marcus Hayes, "He couldn't flex his knees and hips enough to correctly water ski." But after treatment, Cole felt the difference immediately. Three months later, he was running six miles at a time. When he reported to spring training in 2006, he exercised with the team and ran on a treadmill, something his teammates had never seen him do before.

At only 21 years old, constantly fighting injury, he wondered if he might be at the end of his career.

Excited by his new strength, Cole talked with his coaches about a promotion. But the Phillies were concerned about Cole's health and decided to keep him at Clearwater. Just as he had been in high school, Cole was faced with another frustrating setback due to injury. He told interviewer Jeff Passan, "I was totally against it. . . . [It was] just another thing I had to prove to myself and everyone else."

Motivated and stubborn, Cole proved the Phillies wrong. He blazed up the ranks of the minors in 2006. Cole played so well in Clearwater that he skipped the next level of play, double-A, and went straight to the triple-A Red Barons of Scranton/Wilkes-Barre, Pennsylvania, at the end of April.

Phillies assistant general manager Mike Arbuckle (right) announces Cole's upcoming Major League debut at a news conference on May 10, 2006. The Phillies bought out Cole's Minor League contract after his impressive performance on their Scranton/Wilkes-Barre AAA team.

In his first game there, he struck out 14 batters in 7 innings, a new club record. He electrified the crowds, striking out 36 batters in 3 games and giving up only 1 walk and 1 run. The Phillies were so impressed that they called Cole up to the big leagues after only three triple-A games. Cole's Minor League record stands at 14 wins and 4 losses, with an incredible 273 strikeouts in only 35 games pitched.

All Eyes on Hollywood

On May 12, 2006, Cole took the mound with the Phillies for the first time, pitching against the Reds on a chilly, rainy Friday night. Cool-cucumber Cole was not at all nervous about pitching against famous names like boyhood favorite Ken Griffey Jr., but he was nervous about the weather. "I had never pitched a game in the rain in my life, growing up in San Diego," he told interviewer Erin Farrell.

Cole's rainy Major League debut was a splash. He held the Reds scoreless for five straight innings, striking out Ken Griffey Jr. twice. The Phillies went on to win the game, but Cole didn't get credit for the win. His first "W" came against the Arizona Diamondbacks on June 6, when he allowed only 1 run in $5^2/_3$ innings. He even scored a run himself in that game, after getting on base with a walk. Cole's best performance of the season came on August 14, when he shut out the Mets for eight innings. He ended his first Major League season with a solid 145 strikeouts and a 4.08 ERA over $132^1/_3$ innings pitched.

The 2006 season gave fans only a taste of what Cole could do. He pitched his first complete game on April 21,

Cole pitches in his Major League debut on May 12, 2006. He allowed just one hit in five innings, giving the Phillies the start they needed in their 8-4 victory over the Cincinnati Reds.

Cole signs autographs before a game at Philadelphia's Citizens Bank Park. His exciting strikeouts and down-to-earth personality made him an instant hit with Phillies fans.

2007, against the Reds, striking out a career-high 15 batters. In a June 2, 2007, game against the San Francisco Giants, Cole pitched to legendary hitter Barry Bonds. A confident Cole, throwing only his signature changeup, struck out Bonds, statistically the best hitter in the league. By June 12, Cole was the National League leader in wins, and made the National League All-Star Team in July. He led the Phillies to first place in the National League East on September 28, after striking out 13 Washington Nationals. Cole ended the season with 177 strikeouts over $183\,^1/_3$ innings. His ERA of 3.39 was in the top 20 of Major League pitchers.

In a league full of true pros, what makes Cole so good, so special? Most Major League left-handed pitchers use a time-tested formula to strike out batters—throw two fastballs, then get the batter out with a changeup. Cole takes the formula to a new level with his control and variety. Cole throws a four-seam fastball that zooms across the plate at upwards of 90 mph. His wicked curveballs have been clocked at above 70 mph. But his secret weapon, of course, is his changeup.

Phillies catcher Chris Coste told the *Philadelphia City Paper*, "I don't want to use the word 'lazily,' but that is what it does. It looks so hittable and then it just falls off."

Cole's major advantage is his acting skill. Even baseball experts watching him on replay tapes can't tell the difference between his changeup and his fastball delivery. Baseball analyst Mitch Williams explained to the *City Paper*, "Hitters feed off changes they make you make. . . . That is what [Cole] does an exceptional job of: He doesn't show anything." After only three years, Cole's changeup was rated as the most unhittable pitch in the Major Leagues.

Another key to Cole's success is his ability to stay calm no matter how hot the situation. His Phillies teammates call him "Hollywood." The nickname refers both to his California roots and to his unusual comfort in the glaring spotlight of the pitcher's mound. "Hollywood means a lot to this team," Phillies first baseman Ryan Howard told the *City Paper*. "Playing behind him gives us the confidence that he's going to go out there and shut them down." For someone with a medical file thicker than those of most people his age, Cole says his confidence comes from finally being healthy. To maintain that good health, Phillies manager Charlie Manuel set up a simple but strict pitching schedule—Cole pitches only once every five days.

Cole does have his bad days. He said in the MLB web site interview, "You are going to make mistakes, but you have to have the mind-set that you aren't going to repeat them." He makes it a point to hang around with veteran teammates

A Cole Hamels bobblehead

Jimmy Rollins predicted that the Phillies were "the team to beat" in 2007. They won their division that season, thanks in part to these suited-up star players (left to right): Ryan Howard, Cole Hamels, Jimmy Rollins, Brett Myers, and Chase Utley.

who can teach him the most. Almost every game, you can see him huddled on the bench with pitcher Jamie Moyer, the oldest active player in the big leagues. Cole is usually modest in interviews, pointing out how young he is and how far he has to go.

Perhaps Cole's most famous mistake came when he pitched the first game in the National League Division Series (NLDS) versus the Colorado Rockies on October 3, 2007. That day was unusually hot for Philadelphia, and Cole wore a long-sleeved shirt. He was pouring sweat by the second inning, and it affected his grip on the ball. He allowed three runs and three hits in the second. He changed clothes by the third inning and performed better, but the damage was done. The Rockies won the game and went on to win the series.

Every Little Leaguer's Dream

*C*oming off the loss in the 2007 playoffs, the Phillies felt that 2008 was their year. Once again, Cole proved to be a big part of it. Cole pitched his first-ever Major League shutout to the Atlanta Braves on May 15, 2008. On June 5, he pitched another shutout versus his old favorites, the Cincinnati Reds. In the 2008 regular season, Cole fanned 196 batters and chalked up 14 wins. He hoped his career-high $227^{1}/_{3}$ innings pitched that season—the second-highest of any pitcher in the National League—would quiet any more talk about his injuries. His low ERA—only 3.09—was even more dazzling because he pitched in the hitter-friendly Citizens Bank Park, which has a low outfield wall. "His ERA is ridiculous in this stadium," former Atlanta Braves pitcher John Smoltz told Fox Sports. But you'll never catch Hamels complaining about the Phillies' stadium. His strategy is simple: "It doesn't matter how [close] the fence is. They're not supposed to hit the ball."

For the second consecutive year, the Phillies advanced to the playoffs. Cole pitched in the first game against the Milwaukee Brewers in the NLDS. In his first career play-off win, Cole dominated through eight innings, striking out nine. The Phillies went on to win the series, then played the Los Angeles Dodgers in the National League Championship Series (NLCS). Cole pitched—and won—Games 1 and 5, striking out 13 batters in only 14 innings. In his three postseason games, Cole kept opponents to a batting average of just 0.173. That, combined with his NLCS ERA of only 1.93, won Cole the series MVP award. Most importantly, Cole's strong defense gave the Phillies the start they needed to win a trip to the World Series.

Cole pitches against the L.A. Dodgers in Game 5 of the National League Championship Series on October 15, 2008. He held the Dodgers to just one run, clinching the win and NLCS pennant for the Phillies, as well as an MVP trophy for himself.

During Game 1 of the 2008 World Series, Cole struck out the Rays' third baseman Evan Longoria.

Cole pitched the first game of the World Series, against the Tampa Bay Devil Rays. He started the game out right, holding the Rays to only two runs in seven innings. The Phillies won, 3–2. Cole's history-making performance would come on Game 5 the following Monday in Philadelphia.

Hamels pitched in pouring-down rain and still held the Rays to just one run in five innings. When the Rays' Carlos Peña batted in a runner in the sixth inning, the field looked more like a water park than a baseball diamond. The game was called for the first-ever 24-hour rain delay in World Series history. The jersey Cole wore that night now hangs in the National Baseball Hall of Fame.

In addition to a champion-ship ring, Cole also won his own trophy— World Series MVP.

When play resumed on Wednesday, the Phillies finished off the Rays 4–3, winning their first World Series in 28 years. In addition to a championship ring, Cole also won his own trophy — World Series MVP. Cole ruled the postseason with a 4–0 record and a 1.80 ERA.

Cole is one of only five players to win a "double-double" — an MVP trophy in both the National League Championship Series and the World Series. On receiving the World Series trophy, he told reporter Barry Bloom, "Truly, it was my teammates behind me who really helped me through these times. They're the ones who scored the runs." Cole's accomplishment is even more remarkable because 2008 was only his third season in the majors. Baseball experts and Phillies fans alike agreed — their 24-year-old ace was just warming up.

What's Next for Cole Hamels?

*O*n January 18, 2009, the Phillies signed their ace to a three-year, $20.5-million contract. The deal is one of the richest contracts ever for a young pitcher, and expires in time for him to be a free agent. But Cole likes the idea of being a Philly forever. He grew up admiring San Diego's Tony Gwynn, who stayed with the Padres for 20 years. He told interviewers at his contract signing that "sometimes players . . . want to stay with the team that had all of their faith in them and drafted them from the start."

For someone so young, Cole seems to enjoy a mature and stable life. Unlike other young baseball players making headlines and even scandals, Cole and his wife, Heidi, live quietly in the Philadelphia suburb of West Chester. Cole and Heidi Strobel were married on New Year's Eve in 2006, when he was only 23. They met when he was in the minors in Florida. Heidi is a former P.E. teacher and contestant on the reality show *Survivor*, and she appeared in his ballpark on a publicity tour. Cole didn't have any clue she was famous; he just approached her and asked her out. Heidi recalled, "I actually had just moved back to Missouri from L.A. and I told him, totally joking of course, [not] 'unless you plan on flying out to Missouri to take me out.' " Two weeks later, the ever-stubborn Cole showed up in Missouri and took Heidi on their first date. Heidi and Cole don't have any kids yet, but Cole joked in an interview on the MLB web site, "We do have a dog that we're trying to raise the right way." The athletic couple enjoys watching movies, doing yoga, and bike riding.

Cole and Heidi already use their fame and resources to give back to their community. They have participated in fund-raising efforts to help kids through the United Nations' children's fund UNICEF, to help homeless animals through the Society for the Prevention of Cruelty to Animals (SPCA)

Cole and his wife Heidi talk to reporters. A former P.E. teacher, Heidi is working on her Ph.D. from Drexel University. She and her sister, Dawn, also started a company, SistasShirts, that makes fitness shirts for women.

of Philadelphia, and to help impoverished and sick people through HomeAID for Africa. They also donated soccer supplies to kids in Thailand after a massive tsunami struck the country in 2007.

Cole and Heidi together started the Hamels Foundation, a charity promoting education for needy kids. Education is

Cole and Heidi . . . are building a girls' school in the African country of Malawi.

important to Cole himself. Both his parents are educators, and Heidi is working on her Ph.D. Cole hopes to go to college one day and get a degree. For now, he and Heidi donate and raise money to help others get a good education. Twenty to thirty percent of all their foundation proceeds each year go directly to a needy inner-city school in Philadelphia.

While Cole and Heidi help kids in town, they also hope to draw attention to the foundation's bigger cause: They are building a girls' school in the African country of Malawi. The southeastern African nation has been devastated by HIV/AIDS and high infant death rates, as well as flooding and deforestation. When Cole and Heidi went on their honeymoon to South Africa in 2007, they realized how severe the situation was. Heidi told interviewer Patrick Gallen, "If you can give education to these girls, that's what's going to help change Africa."

When he's not helping kids halfway across the world, Cole is energizing Phillies fans who had given up hope on winning. The Phillies posted their ten-thousandth loss in 2007 — the most losses by a professional sports team in

On Halloween 2008, the city of Philadelphia honored its World Series Champs with a victory parade. Schools were closed and crowds of fans packed downtown streets to catch a glimpse of their favorite Phillies, like Cole and fellow starting pitcher Brett Myers.

history. So, not surprisingly, the town went crazy when Cole and his team won the biggest trophy in all of baseball.

As the pressure mounted for the 2009 season, Cole admitted to interviewer Patrick Gallen, "After you win a World Series, people expect a little bit more." His new goal was to get 20 wins in a season. Certainly Cole has the dedication, the humility, and the nasty changeup to do it. This old-school lefty will be fun for Phillies fans to watch for a long time to come.

CAREER STATISTICS

YR	Team	GS	W	L	IP	H	R	ER	HR	BB	K	ERA
2006	Phillies	23	9	8	132.1	117	66	60	19	48	145	4.08
2007	Phillies	28	15	5	183.1	163	72	69	25	43	177	3.39
2008	Phillies	33	14	10	227.1	193	89	78	28	53	196	3.09
Career		84	38	23	543.0	473	227	207	72	144	518	3.43

(GS=Games started, W=Wins, L=Losses, IP=Innings pitched, H=Hits, R=Runs, ER=Earned runs, HR=Home runs allowed, BB=Bases on balls, K=Strikeouts, ERA=Earned-run average)

Cole Hamels gives "The Top Ten List" on The David Letterman Show, *November 2008*

1983   Colbert Michael Hamels is born on December 27 in San Diego, California.

1999   He joins the baseball team at Rancho Bernardo High School in San Diego.

2002   Cole is chosen by the Philadelphia Phillies in the first round of the Major League draft; he graduates from Rancho Bernardo High School.

2003   Cole begins his career in Phillies' Minor League teams. He starts with the single-A Lakewood BlueClaws in New Jersey and is promoted to the advanced-A Clearwater Threshers in Florida. He wins the Paul Owens Award for Best Minor League Pitcher in the Philadelphia Phillies Organization.

2004   Cole is out for most of the season with an elbow injury.

2005   Cole plays for Clearwater and the double-A Phillies in Reading, Pennsylvania, but is out for much of the season with a broken hand and injured back.

2006   Cole plays for Clearwater and is promoted to the triple-A Red Barons in Scranton/Wilkes-Barre, Pennsylvania. He makes his first Major League appearance on May 12 and has his first Major League win on June 6. Cole marries Heidi Strobel on December 31.

2007   Cole appears in the All-Star Game on July 10. The Phillies become the first professional sports team with 10,000 losses on July 15. Phillies lose to the Colorado Rockies in the National League Division Series; Hamels pitches in Game 1 of the series on October 3.

2008   Phillies beat the L.A. Dodgers to win the National League Championship on October 15; Hamels wins NLCS MVP. Phillies beat the Tampa Bay Devil Rays to win the World Series on October 29; Hamels is named the World Series MVP.

2009   Phillies sign Hamels to a 3-year, $20.5-million contract on January 18.

FURTHER READING

Books

Staff of Philadelphia Inquirer and Daily News. *Champions!: A Look Back at the Phillies Triumphant 2008 Season.* Philadelphia: Camino Books, Inc., 2008.

Zumnuich, Fran. *Phantastic! The 2008 Champion Philadelphia Phillies.* Chicago: Triumph Books, 2008.

Works Consulted

Bamberger, Michael. "Just 24, Old-school Lefty Hamels Figures to Be Key Series Factor." *Sports Illustrated.* October 22, 2008. http://sportsillustrated.cnn.com/2008/writers/michael_bamberger/10/21/cole.hamels/index.html

Beale, E. James. "We Need A Hero." *Philadelphia City Paper.* August 19, 2008. http://www.citypaper.net/articles/2008/08/21/we-need-a-hero

Becker, Matt. *Yahoo! Sports,* "Philadelphia (19–15) at Cincinnati (23–12) Preview" http://sports.yahoo.com/mlb/preview?gid=260512117

Bloom, Barry M. *WorldSeries.com 08,* "Perfect Hamels Is World Series MVP" http://mlb.mlb.com/news/article.jsp?ymd=20081029&content_id=3653295&vkey=ps2008news&fext=.jsp&c_id=mlb&partnerId=rss_mlb

ESPN: *MLB Play-offs 2008,* "Hamels, Who Was 4–0 in Postseason, Wins World Series MVP" http://article.wn.com/view/2008/10/30/Hamels_who_was_40_in_postseason_wins_World_Series_MVP/

Farrell, Erin. "Q&A: Phillies LHP Cole Hamels." *Sporting News.* February 22, 2007. http://www.sportingnews.com/yourturn/viewtopic.php?t=180210

Gallen, Patrick. "First Lady of the Phils: an Interview with Heidi Hamels." *Philadelphia Phillies Examiner.* January 9, 2009. http://www.examiner.com/x-1164-Philadelphia-Phillies-Examiner~y2009m1d9-Heidi-Hamels-interview-Part-one

———. "Starting Spring Early: the Cole Hamels Interview." *Philadelphia Phillies Examiner.* January 12, 2009. http://www.examiner.com/x-1164-Philadelphia-Phillies-Examiner~y2009m1d12-Starting-spring-early-The-Cole-Hamels-interview

Gennaria, Mike. *Phillies World Series Champions 2008.* "Hamels to Have Surgery on Left Hand" http://philadelphia.phillies.mlb.com/news/article.jsp?ymd=20050201&content_id=937908&vkey=news_phi&fext=.jsp&c_id=phi

Hayes, Marcus. "Delving into Cole Hamels' Holistic Approach." *Philadelphia Daily News.* September 30, 2008. http://www.philly.com/dailynews/sports/20080930_Delving_into_Cole_Hamels__holistic_approach.html

Jenkins, Lee. "Phillies Prospect Has Stuff Dreams Are Made of." *New York Times.* May 23, 2006. http://mysite.verizon.net/heyjude421/chf/nytimes.html

JockBio: "Cole Hamels Biography" http://www.jockbio.com/Bios/Hamels/Hamels_bio.html

Major League Baseball: "Q&A with the Phillies' Cole Hamels" http://mlbplayers.mlb.com/content/printer_friendly/mlbpa/y2007/m04/d13/c1896039.jsp

Mandel, Ken. *Phillies World Series Champions 2008,* "Phillies Select Hamels in First Round" http://philadelphia.phillies.mlb.com/news/article.jsp?ymd=20020604&content_id=41807&vkey=news_phi&fext=.jsp&c_id=phi

Passan, Jeff. *Yahoo! Sports.* "King Cole" http://sports.yahoo.com/mlb/news?slug=jp-hamels051806&prov=yhoo&type=lgns

Salisbury, Jim. "Hamels, Phils Agree to 3-year, $20.5M Deal." *The Philadelphia Inquirer.* January 18, 2009. http://www.philly.com/philly/sports/20090118_Hamels__Phils_agree_to_3-year___20_5M_deal.html

Tennis, Mark. *ESPN Rise.* "California Has Most Players in World Series" http://sports.espn.go.com/highschool/rise/baseball/news/story?id=3654991

Verducci, Tom. "Dear America, Wish You Were Here." *Sports Illustrated.* November 3, 2008. http://vault.sportsillustrated.cnn.com/vault/article/magazine/MAG1147433/3/index.htm

Zolecki, Todd. "Hamels a Phil for 3 years — and Counting." *The Philadelphia Inquirer.* January 19, 2009. http://www.philly.com/inquirer/sports/20090119_Hamels_a_Phil_for_3_years_-_and_counting.html

On the Internet

Cole Hamels Official Web Site
    http://www.colehamels.com

SI Kids: *MLB Players,* "Cole Hamels"
    http://www.sikids.com/baseball/mlb/players/7509/

INDEX

All-Star Game   17
Arbuckle, Mike   14
Atlanta Braves   20
Blalock, Hank   7
Bonds, Barry   17
changeup   5, 6, 8, 9, 11, 16, 17–18
chiropractor   13
Cincinnati Reds   15, 16, 17, 20
Citizens Bank Park   6, 17, 20
Clearwater Threshers   12–13
Colorado Rockies   19
Coste, Chris   18
curveball   18
draft, Major League   5, 11
Dugaf, Dr. Christopher   13
ERA   11, 12, 15, 20, 21, 23
fastball   6, 8, 10, 17–18
Fronek, Dr. Jan   10
Furtak, Mark   8
Griffey, Ken, Jr.   15
Gwynn, Tony   24
Hall of Fame   23
Hamels, Amanda (mother)   5–6
Hamels, Cole
    birth of   5
    charity work of   25–26
    childhood of   5–7
    contracts of   11, 24
    education of   5, 6–9
    first MLB game   15
    first MLB win   15
    in high school   5, 6–11
    hobbies of   6, 25
    injuries of   9, 10–11, 12–13, 18
    in Little League   7
    in Major League   15–19, 20–23,
        24–35
    marriage of   24

in Minor League   12–14
as MVP   21, 23
in training   12–13
Hamels, Gary (father)   5–6, 10
Hamels, Heidi Strobel (wife)   24–
    26
Hamels Foundation   26
Hoffman, Trevor   6, 8
"Hollywood" (nickname)   17
House, Tom   10
Howard, Ryan   17, 19
L.A. Dodgers   20
Lakewood BlueClaws   12
Malawi   26
Manuel, Charlie   17
Meadowbrook Middle School   6
Milwaukee Brewers   20
Moyer, Jamie   19
Myers, Brett   19, 27
National League Playoffs   19, 20–
    21
New York Mets   15
Rancho Bernardo High School   6–
    9, 10–11
Rollins, Jimmy   19
San Diego Padres   6, 8, 24
Saunders, Tony   10
scouts   5, 8, 10–11
Scranton/Wilkes-Barre Red Barons
    13
shutouts   15, 20
Smoltz, John   20
strikeouts   15, 17
surgery   10
Tampa Bay Devil Rays   4, 22, 23
Utley, Chase   19
Washington Nationals   17
World Series   4, 21, 22, 23, 27
World Series MVP   23